ScorpiGem Business Expansion

A Company co-owned by Geri Townsley who is known for her creative talent

Authored by Geri R. Townsley
PUBLISHED by ScorpiGem Books

An imprint of ScorpiGem Limited
Palmerston North, 4412
New Zealand

Copyright ©2017 Geri R.TOWNSLEY

Want to read more Geri R. Townsley
https://grtownsley.wordpress.com
https://scorpigemblog.wordpress.com/

Book Edition License Notes
This book is licensed for your personal enjoyment only. This book may not be re-sold or given away to other people. If you would like to share this book with another person, please purchase an additional copy for each person you share it with. If you're reading this book and did not purchase it, or it was not purchased for your use only, then you should purchase your own copy. Thank you for respecting the author's work.

ScorpiGem Business Expansion 1
A Company co-owned by Geri Townsley who is known for her creative talent 1
.... 3
Executive Summary 3
    Management Team 7
    Geri Townsley's writing work 9
    Albie Merani and the Deathly Storm (Book One) 19
The ScorpiGem Business Plan 23
    Marketing Plan 26
    About Global warming and climate change 30
    Financial Plan 35
    Products 40

Executive Summary

Travel to the Bahamas is too expensive. However, lawyer's there want 25% of Geri Townsley's assets and that's a rip-off. Our business only needs eighty thousand dollars to cover startup costs therefore, I have written a book.

I suffered an injury in London 7/7, 2005 at Tavistock Square by the bus explosion luckily I survived the explosion but still to this day suffer from back and neck pain and you will also not find me listed as a passenger on that damn bus as no one bothered to asked me for my name. Well they were too busy anyway. This is why I forgot the location of my safe and all that is required is for me to travel to the Bahamas?

ScorpiGem is committed to delivering and taking full advantage of world Energy market that will allow Power Companies and small to medium sized village's to very large cities access to our new technology to generate zero emission electricity.

Why we will be successful, ScorpiGem Limited enjoys an expression of satisfaction and encouragements are numerous, and we intend to take advantage of this to grow in the marketplace with more unique and effective products. Based on the attached financial projections, we believe that this venture represents a sound business proposition.

Palmerston North artistic writer Geri Townsley known for her writing and filmmaking talent has a unique opportunity to bring her characters to life through her film 'The Cataclysm – Dark Horizons'. A science fiction thriller set in a dual red dwarf star system. This idea was after a recent dram I had were I was on-board a star ship which enters a dual red dwarf star system, this lead me to come up with the science fiction story The Cataclysm:

The Cataclysm is set on an old alien abandon space cube orbiting a star about 500 light years from Earth which is still mulling over in my mind.

Recently received a quick call from Mrs. Peterson and she has confirmed my safe is at their Nassau Bahamas branch. Hence, this is awesome news. ❖ This is why we have travel to the Bahamas but it is too expensive to travel there. However, lawyer's there want 25% of my assets and that's a rip-off. Business only needs eighty thousand dollars to cover startup costs.

Another project ScorpiGem Technology Limited is committed to taking full advantage of world Energy market that will allow Power Companies and small to medium sized village's to very large cities access to our new technology to generate zero emission electricity.

Our company can be characterized as a technology business and we are committed to delivering and taking full advantage of the decline of the world computer industry and now with the support of companies like PB Tech and Anyware NZ and the move to Mini PCs now allows us to grow our market size.

Our primary objective is to drive prices in New Zealand down by first selling our own brand Mini and Micro PCs.

Our secondary objective is, to carry out the following:

Target small business owners would be the primary target for mini PC sales that fits on the back of your computer monitor.

All that's needed are external hard drive and DVD/Blu-ray drive. In addition, a low cost keyboard/mouse pack.

If the business grows, we will have to employ staff.

Reason why PC sales have plummeted is due to people no longer have enough funds to pay over $1,000 for a brand new PC. Whereas Mini PCs cost $799 and that includes 24" monitor, keyboard/mouse and we have two models: one comes with Windows 10 Home x64 install and other model comes with Zorin Core x64 a free operating system that has the look and feel of Windows 7.

When someone purchases our Mini PC all they have to do is set it up, turn the PC on and wait for the pre-installed OS to boot up there you go assembly is not required.

An advantage of going with a voip service rather than a conventional land line is to cost benefit of $50 - 10 = $40 monthly saving plus Talk2 phone calls can be routed via their app to smartphones.

Our biggest seller is going to be our very own ScorpiGem branded 55inch (3840*2160) Ultra HD smart television. They will sell for $1,295 (Inc. GST) and they come with 3-year factory backed warranty. The import cost is $565 (including shipping cost), so the profit margin is $698 times 100 equals $69,800 tax paid profit in first year of sales.

We will so be the only company to assemble in New Zealand our own branded Micro personal computers by directly import parts and components from Mainland China. We plan to hire two to four people to help us assemble our PCs here in Palmerston North and they will be paid $18 per hour.

We also plan to purchase a workshop and office containers from China, which will allow us to expend our work and storage areas.

Business Location

ScorpiGem Limited's business headquarters are located in Palmerston North, New Zealand.

Legal Business Description

The legal form of ScorpiGem Limited is a Limited Liability Company. We chose the Limited Liability Company form because it offers lower tax and better protection for directors and shareholders alike.

Strategic Alliances & Potential Partners

ScorpiGem Limited is very interested in relationships with major companies in the energy industry. Like;

AGL (Australian Gas & Light) an Australian bases electricity & gas supplier.

PowerCo a New Zealand base electricity supplier.

GE (General Electric Corporation) makes gas turbines, generators & jet engines.

Note: One major benefit for GE would be the exclusive worldwide manufacturing rights (for the term of the worldwide patent).

Objectives

To build Gen Townsley's soon to be patented high powered (and extremely efficient) generator technology for the global energy markets!

To sell and install security and networking products around the Manawatu region.

To sell 55inch (3840*2160) UHD Televisions with USB, HDMI, VGA and DVBT all over New Zealand mostly via Trademe.

We can import products made for us in China directly into Australia and with a deal with the likes of Digicor they can help us expand our business deeper into Australia too.

Licencing Fees

Our licence fees are as follows:

Manufacturing licencing fee: 5% pa. Royalty fee: 15% pa.

Capital Requirements

Our business needs $250,000 to develop our new electronic, mini PC and networking business.

Marketing and Promotion - Prnz, Google & Stuff, Marketing Materials, Voip business phone line, setup webhosting account, registration our company, pay PNCC for a certificate of compliance, purchase printer ink & paper. Order software, laptop and table, computer chair and new monitor. However, we have to order Mini PCs and various parts to keep in stock.

Management Team

Consists of;

Geri Townsley

Palmerston North based Geri Townsley operates ScorpiGem Limited is known for her creative talent, she once worked in the movie industry, primarily based in Sydney Australia. This meant her skills are still great even after being out of the industry for a while. Geri is the inventor of the Torq Velocity generator.

Her other project is her new film 'The Cataclysm – Dark Horizons'. A science fiction thriller set in a dual red dwarf star system. This idea was after a recent dram I had were I was on-board a star ship which enters a dual red dwarf star system, this lead me to come up with the science fiction story The Cataclysm is set on an old alien abandon space cube orbiting a star about 500 light years from Earth. Where aliens unknowingly release an evil entity from its confinement whom come under attack. A Team of ex-solders on-board an experimental starship arrive at the disused cube in orbit around a small gas giant orbiting a red dwarf star. The entity ends up destroying Earth and its solar system. However, it's not a where there is a time agent trapped in the outer reaches of the solar system new nebular.
Inspiration for this film come from Star Trek V: The Final Frontier is a 1989 American science fiction film released by Paramount Pictures.

In Australia back in the mid-90s she was offered a three movie deal which lead to six movies, including: Giving Brian Brown a hand (please excuse the pun) with his movie 'Two Hands'. When Heath Ledger & she had arrived a bit late at Avalon Beach in Sydney Australia, I rushed to the sea and scooped up a handful of salt water after drinking it. Heath said. "For the life of me, I've never seen anyone doing that before."

If you want to know who came up with the idea of breaking open the safe in the movie

"The Score," well it was Geri Townsley. We sealed the door with a product called Knead It (made by Selleys), Bob used a thermic lance to cut a hole in the middle of the safe, he filled it with water, and soon afterwards, he inserted a detonator. Backing off with a remote already in his right hand, a flick of a switch, and whoosh the door blew off, and everyone on set was amazed!

Being a permanent resident of Australia and having both American & British citizenship gives Geri Townsley's company access to Australia, Europe, and Canada/USA.

Peter Donachie

His background consists of more than 10 years of experience in sales and distribution and warehouse operations.

Geri Townsley's writing work

The Cataclysm

The year is 2061, former Captain Mark Diller is a man not to be tangled with recently retired from ten years in the army, and now works as a security consultant for a privately owned high-tech research company based south of his home in a nearby Australian city of Sydney walks out of building one. Before hoping in to his car, a white four-door city type car he looks around the facility surrounded by security fences and partly surrounded by various warehouses with an old factory to its rear. Satisfied all was ok hops into his car once past the security gate a quick nod to the guard in the booth and after a few minutes pulls into his driveway on entering his house kisses his wife of ten years on left cheek they eat a meal each. Watches some television since both had to head into work early settled in for the night.

Later the following day head scientist Alex Church strolling along the hallway wearing a usual white coat catches sight of Mark exiting his office for a bite to eat is delayed by Alex who interrupted his train of thought and as they enter the lunch room their boss Shawn Fontaine man in his thirties was a demanding boss and when it came to his business dealing and his staff was sitting on his own at a table waiting for his meal to arrive. The cook Louise aka Lou to everyone working at the complex saw them sitting down put their meals on a tray and promptly brought their previously ordered meals over to them.

Head scientist Alex Church was excited that tomorrow morning they were going to test the new engines amazed at finding such a bright individual especially considering that man was in his early twenties and is straight out of university. Almost a clone of Kelly Johnston the man who created the Blackbird and now they too have such an amazing talent in their grasp.

Mark heads back to his office and as he was about to sit his phone sings and sings. His boss who requires his presence heads upstairs to his boss' office. Who hands him a piece of paper. "Organize security for the engine test tomorrow."

Mark nods his approval Shawn without a word-spoken waves Mark off walks back to his own office presses a button of a terminal screen and after a monument a man appears on his display screen. The men agree to a time -call ends-.

Mark's head pops up from his monitor's screen after hearing heavy footsteps heading in the direction of his office. A security guard almost out of breath with a look of concern on his face walks briskly into his office stops, takes a breather. There's a white van out the back of their facility. Marks stands, grabs binoculars from shelf, security guard follows him along hallway and outside via a side door.

Mark and the security guard scamper over to a nearby wall. No markings, windows bar driver's window are dark the man looks familiar? Takes photo sends photo to his computer.

The driver spots something in the distance as a dark hair man head appears over the top of the wall closes window turns van around and drives away, both men return inside the building by they had come from.

The following day at 5:30am, Mark arrives at work and parks in his usual spot walks over to a truck parked in front of warehouse two with fellow staff hanging around while a man pushes something covered with a tarp onto a loading cube. He closes the door hops in the transport truck Mark sees a company pickup truck parked in a great lot.

They soon arrive at an area authorized to do the engine tests an old disused quarry outside of the city after an hour of setting up. Alex connects a generator to the engine. He pushes a button on the consult and whoosh the engine fired instantly to life with flames spit out its exhaust the just an afterglow.

Shawn saunters over and pats the kid (Ray) on his left shoulder and shakes both he and Alex's hand. Claps all round. All that's needed now is complete the core device and that energy device, and then they are finally ready for "Project Alpha."

Alex shuts the engine down while his aids load the engine back in the truck. While the men secure the cube to the trucks rear Mark caught a glint in the edge of his right eye. It's that damn van again.

Taps boss on right shoulder. Removes his weapon but before he could approach the van the squeal of tires alerts him the van has sped away putting his weapon way returns to his boss' right side.

Before Mark could reply he hops back into the pickup truck he last used and before he could take off the passenger door opened. Lou hops Mark knew full well what she used to do for a living floors the gas pedal takes off in pursuit after the white van. Catching up to, the van Mark slows down wanting not to be seen past one City Street to another the white van slows and pulls into a driveway of large warehouse complex. The man hops out and walks through the main entrance disappearing deeper into the building. Mark reaches into the glovebox for a notepad and pen takes note of the business name and address. "Advance Research Group," Looks around area. "Anderson Street." what appears to be moments the pickup with Mark still at the wheel returns to their company's facility after entering the main building via its main entrance door they saunter straight up to their boss and inform him who were spying on them?

Later on while the team were at a local bar celebrating their recent success Lou notices a man looking constantly at them she heads to the toilet after exiting and while returning to their table she decides to approach the one ninety centimeter tall man. The athletic built man tells her to get lost but she refuse to walk away the man pushes her to the floor. Mark saw that and rushes to her aid but he was too slow. Lou got to here feet and within seconds pins the man to the floor. Who was this guy? Mark searches his pocket and finds a security pass "ADG" again what are those guys up to then as Lou lets go of the man he shoves Lou into Mark's open arm runs at fast as his feet could carry him straight outside. Mark gave chase by as he sprinted outside the man had vanished into the darkness. Lou walks to his side and takes position of the security pass time she found out what ADG were doing.

That very night or to be more precise the early hours Lou outfitted in dark clothing approached ADG's rear fence slips over and all the way to the rear security door a swipe of the card, the door unlocks a quick look around. None around the guards are on their tea break saunters inside looks for security cameras slips past them and upstairs to the main office heads. She spot the manager's office but the door was locked slips out of her satchel some tools make short work of the lock enters the office locates a computers terminal removes a USB pass key, she searches from file to file but one peaks her interest "Project Alpha". As she copies the related file to her USB key she hears footsteps in the hallway coming in her direction, she wipes her brow. File copied rushing into the nearby closet a beam of a torch casts into the room but the guard see nothing closes and locks the door. Lou see it time for here to leave and as she walks into the hall way the guard sees her sneaking around rushes over but she was too swift for him and he falls to the floor she then drags the man into the office and makes her way back outside and into the darkness beyond. The following morning she strolls into Mark's office with the flash driver in her right hand, she hands it over to and after scanning the drive, a look of concerned all over his face "Project Alpha." Holly hell someone is spying on them!

The following day inside the large warehouse the boss and Alex are testing the core device and when a man runs at a brisk pace from the smaller warehouse he crashes into an invisible wall. After getting to his feet waves his arms in the air but nothing was there. He then races into the larger warehouse; Alex immediately realizes what he is on about, the shield works perfectly.

A few weeks later Alex and three of his fellow scientists and Marks own security personnel all onboard the ships they take off and head into orbit, where a large experiment starship was waiting for them to arrive. They one by one dock with the ship it then activates the core device designed to twist space and then an energy beam comes out in front of the ship, which opens up an artificial wormhole.

After an hour's travel, the ship enters a binary star system with two red dwarfs orbiting each other on finding an old alien abandon space cube in orbit around a small gas giant in the system, the ship docks to a docking ring. They soon come under attack by a group of unknown aliens who are trying to open a security vault whom also were not aware that an evil alien entity was inside the vault, an explosion later by the aliens meant the entity was released it strikes out at the aliens but it leaves to human crew along. No one noticed gold and platinum stored within the large but secure vault.

The aliens after losing the fire fight back off and return to their ship whom then head to Earth and land near a disused airfield near Schofields NSW Australia while the Australian defence force while out on maneuvers near Schofields receives an executive order they arrive on the scene. The commander barks some orders to his lieutenant who sends out tanks and soldiers to investigate the alien ship parked on a nearby as they approach the craft it opens fire destroying several army vehicles, they return fire as flames rise around the ship dissipates leaving the alien ship totally unharmed.

All of a sudden, an experimental tank with experimental rail run mounted to its rear arrives the alien ship flies high into the air but the tank opens fires the shell penetrates the ship's hull an explosion seen by all on the ground with cheers all round. Nevertheless, before anyone could investigate the ship, the evil entity arrives and hits out in anger at the alien ship it glows and after a few moments explodes destroying Earth and then the entire solar system flinging the evil entity into deep space.

***

Back at the cube; one man looking at a display screen taps his commander on his shoulder the both of them see the supernova explosion the pack up and return to the solar system but Earth is gone
- only thing left is a beautiful nebular.

On return to the nebular the ship's AI announces to the commander he has found an unknown vessel deep inside the nebular. The ship activates its shield and after a search deep inside the nebular, the ship activates a tractor beam and the unknown vessel was brought inside to the landing bay. Mark along with Alex and three security personnel wait while a man and woman brings over a set of stairs. A man after a few seconds opens the access hatch and on boarding Mark orders two security personal to search the rest of the ship while Alex, a female security agent and himself head to the bridge. On entering Alex had a quick look around but could not bring the ship to life, ships power core is offline.

Mark's radio crackles, one of the two security personnel sent off to search the rest of the ship has found something in the ship's center Mark, Alex, and the security agent head to the ship center where they soon locate a container must like an Egyptian sarcophagus, Alex has a looks at the display English? He turns to Mark and states they need their tech guy to have a look at the device. One his arrival he plays around with the touch screen display and after a few minutes the lid opened reveling a human woman inside the protected area. On freeing her she motions to one man who hands here a bottle of water, she then informs them she is a 'Time Guardian'. Mark quizzes her about the alien entity and she then informs him that that entity is a threat to the entire galaxy.

She looks at the display on her wrist the ship is unresponsive the explosion has badly damaged her ship and the gold and platinum which is need for time travel but it's beyond repair. The only avenue left to them now is to return to the alien cube, retrieve the related materials, and then reconfigure their ship for time travel.

On their arrival back at the alien cube the ship docks with the cube and while the guys plodded along one hallway, then another after thirty minutes they arrived back at the vault and before they could take possession of the related material, six of the aliens still remained safely secured within the vault a fire fight ensued. Mark's team could not eliminate them, so they have to find another way into the vault.
One of Mark's team then proposed after peering into the back of the vault, he sees what walks looks like a hidden door, then another man strides over to

Mark who found tunnel that leads to vault's rear. Mark then ordered three of his team to keep the guys safely ensconced in the vault why he and his guys find another way inside the vault.

About thirty minutes of trudging through a water logged the tunnel, one man who takes point sees a narrow opening that leads into another tunnel after crawling through to the other side. They finally see a door and on entering the vault, Mark spots his team members he signals to them to open fire, Mark and his team take positions near boxes and other hardware, the team after short firefight eliminates the remaining aliens. They then retrieved the gold and platinum and head immediately back to their ship as the entered the cargo area engineers walks over and he suggest they should take the gold and platinum to the engineering workshop. Once inside the engineers' got to work and with help of the time agent a new power core is built after installing it in the ship mid sections were the current core is located, the engineers' install the device, and once connected to the ship's system the ship is now ready for time travel.

After an hour or more of testing their new core device within the confines of the star system solar system, the ships AI detects the entity's energy signature, the ship warps over and just as they near the alien's whom attacked them home world, the shield drops and as the entity strikes out the alien's home world the planet explodes. A pulse of energy strikes their ship a surge causes the new power core to go offline, the evil entity notices that and gives chase, they head into the asteroid belt swinging pass one asteroid then another but the entity was still on their tail.

The ships drive engines kicked in a burst of light later and the ship enters the star systems Ort cloud. The entity is still on their case while the team repairs the core the ship swings past a large comet the ships drive engines burst into life once again and the comet let fly nonetheless the entity casually flicks it to one side. Just as the ship engines kicked in again the core comes to life just as the entity slams hard into their sip the shields flicks it into deep space beyond the star system's Oort cloud. The ship with the entity still on their tail swings around the star system's yellow sun the entity catches up to them.

Mark's team see that, his second in charge walks over to him and suggests they head at maximum velocity to the nearest quasar black hole, the lead scientist thinks they could entrap the entity in a tractor beam that his team had been working on in secret. Mark nods his approval and with the help of the time guardian agent, they drag the evil entity behind their ship all the way to the quasar on the arrival. The ship loops around the black hole as evil entity struggles to release itself the back hole grips the entity hard the ship drops the tractor beam after what seems like hours or days pass. The black hole's resilient grip the ship warps and folds space, forming a wormhole the ship is flung hard within, instead of arriving back near Earth in the present, they're now one year before the supernova explosion.

The ship cloaks itself so that no one on Earth can see their ship they head immediately back to the star system on their arrival at mysterious cube they prevent the aliens from releasing the evil entity from its confinement. Takes vault with evil entity with in, to nearest quasar black hole, flings the vault straight into the black hole as the vault crumples the entity tries to escape but the back holes has a firm hold. The gold within goes nuclear the resulting explosion shoots the ship around the black hole to near the speed of light on their exit they soon find out they are back once again in the present. With both the Earth and the alien home world – Garmondee completely restored.

Albie Merani and the Deathly Storm (Book One)

Everything looked safe, felt safe to Albie Merani.

In the spring of 1854 -- As a whirling maelstrom of strong winds in the southern Larnis Ocean formed a blue light burst from within, then a ship a long triple massed steamer appeared out of nowhere to burst beyond it's normal speed. As people walking along a beach close to a small provincial town of Parvis Beach sprinted out of the way after seeing a ship coming toward them. Seeing jagged rocks on the horizon, the ship swerved in time to miss them by fractions of an inch. Lightning crossed the sky with strong winds bearing down on her she was forced toward Parvis Beach's pristine beach with golden sand across its surface. People after hearing a loud horn brought them on the scene to help passengers and the ship's crew to disembark from their beautiful but grounded ship.

The planet Zaron is an unstable world, where continents continuously drift along to, forever rove nomadically move across land and sea in search of new places in which to reside. Zaron is a united planet people there are encouraged to live their dreams.

Many years later in early summer young scientist Albie Merani and his friends struggling to manage his Mag-Ve team Zaron's leading handball game on steroids, Finds things have gone astray, assaulted by two eerie and mysterious men when he returns from an unexpected trip. Albie must locate his missing girlfriend but was she kidnapped or has something happened to her? All before a malevolent storm jeopardizes the safety and security of those, he loves..

Synopsis

Albie Merani the captain of Hamarchi Phoenix and once his business meeting is over two men, who were spying on him, suddenly came out of nowhere and began to attack him, his adventure turns into something thrilling and dangerous, as he tries to head them of, heading on vacation with his family away, their lab is broken into, returning discovered computers and his experimental power module, gone the thieves build devices, their actions cause a mysterious and violent storm which slams into the town of Garris, resulting in flooding and damage in low-lying areas.

Albie's mother (Genari Merani) and his sister Genora are staying at a hotel in Parvis Beach, while out walking around the town and upon returning. She spotted two men walking out onto the footpath from the back of the hotel, she took a photo of one of them, she turns to her daughter, Genora where they raced back into their hotel made their way back to their room. - Genari had a quick look around, but she couldn't find anything missing?

As Brad and Nick looked down from Walt's balcony after forcing the door open they both saw a white van turning left on to Browley Road, and as they looked at each other, looking puzzled they couldn't understand why Albie (Merani) was one step ahead of them, they had no idea that Steve was double dealing, acting as an informant for Albie.

Traveling on the train heading back to Hamarchi Albie meets up with an engineer that could solve all his problems and after arriving back he and Raine spend four days in Garris. They join a tour group make their way into the haunted warehouse, they tour guide went missing, Albie and Raine find him, but he is dead - Albie learns later on that the man looked like him.

Someone breaks into Albie parent's lab and steal experimental technology to build several devices and after they started using the devices, unaware that a mysterious storm is on the way; ends up causing severe flooding and damage to buildings in low-lying areas of the town of Garris. They use the storm to their advantage, where they break into the Hamarchi Gold Reserve.

On Albie and Raine's (his partner of two years) return to Garris traveling in a six-wheeled vehicle, with parts of Garris flooded, makes his way to his cousin's house Raine went into the house, where a man in a jetpack came out of nowhere and attacked him. He threw a stone hitting a valve them man flew away in an uncontrolled manner Albie gave chase not realizing what had happened to Raine, returning he couldn't locate her - she went missing. Albie heads to the stadium to locate Agent Garmardi, but Raine was not there either - where on Zaron had she gone?

Raine had beforehand fallen from the back deck of Albie cousin's house, crashed into the water, but managed to struggle onto a log that floated by, floated over to the house on the hill, reaching the house grabs hold of the trellis climbed up where she managed to crawl over and onto the rear balcony. The following morning she awakes to find herself in bed in a strange room - with phone lines down and unaware she's now in the house on the hill.

Sooner rather than later the storm slams into the outer reaches of Hamarchi Albie has to locate Raine his girlfriend, then head by transport train to Hamerton located on the Isle of Berge. Where undercover Agent Jarnie Zarton finally locates the bad guys and they are on the island, partying up like crazy, he manages to con his way on-board their boat.

Jarnie manages to hack into their computer system, gleamed as much data as he could, transferring the data to a flash drive. Exits the boat, luckily for him he wasn't spotted, all the while managing to offload it to Albie.

Jarnie informs Albie as to where the bad guys are – they're located in an old warehouse complex on the nearby peninsula. Albie made his way back to where they agents were -- they all climb back into his vehicle. They reach warehouse one and after entering, Albie manages to disable the equipment and shortly after the storm dissipates – before it slams headlong into the city of Hamarchi.

Albie along with four agents from the SDIS are on a ship is in pursuit of the bad guys boat, but the bad guys launch a drone it then fires two missiles at the SDIS ship and both misses miss the SDIS ship. The captain then sends Albie and Agent Garmardi outside with portable rod launchers and both of them target the drone, firing rod weapons at the drone, later on after a moment or two it exploded.

A drone that was flying back from a mission stops and records the action. Shortly after a blue door appeared ahead of the bad guy's boat, where they disappear through and a short time later, the SDIS ship pulled closer and closer to the event - their ship disappeared through the event -- the event then dissipated.

The ScorpiGem Business Plan

Geri Townsley co-owner of ScorpiGem Limited now has a unique opportunity to bring this Torq motor generator project to life.

What are you developing?

After an accident in early 2006 and after a dream it drove Geri Townsley back into development once again. She has always been a creative and driven person. However, our company has not been able to find any funds to develop a proof of concept of Geri Townsley's new motor generator idea.

Over the past few years she's been building up support on Twitter and with the anticipation of eventually building a prototype motor generator became apparent clear to us about four years ago what this device should be. We introduce the Torq motor generator project, a highly efficient motor with built-in controller, which uses lasers to turn the motor's rotor at high speed but we need material tools and hardware to carry out this experiment.

Anyway, it looks like people want more and though obtaining funding these days is difficult, as people in both New Zealand and on the Internet want to see a fully functioning device built before they agree to any funding requests. The big problem is that sites like those morons at Kickstarter whom won't allow experiment products to be listed on their site. Makes funding an experiment product hard to fund as a proof of concept model is expensive to construct.

What We Need & What You Get?

We now need in order to construct a proof-of-concept model, which requires the purchase of a specialist laboratory furnace (needed to anneal metal parts for strengthening, pay cad designer their cost to produce 3D version of our design so that their company can print metal and plastic parts in their 3D printers.

Stage 1

The cost to construct a proof of concept is $250,000. Funding

from crowdfunding will help with paying for parts, electronic components and construction, any extra raised will go towards; tools, testing equipment (like an oscilloscope), and purchase a machinery and hardware. Pay for marketing, press releases, website development, apply for patenting and pay for compliance testing, etc.

Stage 2

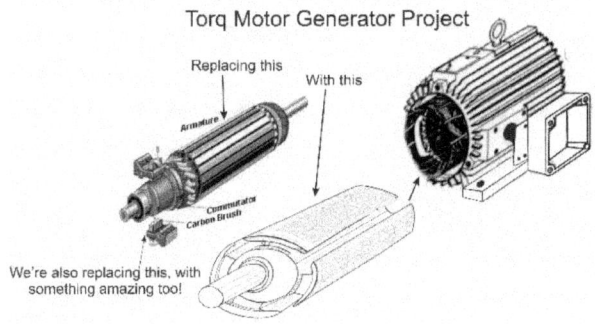

Start limited production to test the motor generator in the New Zealand market; like homes and business to see how each motor runs.

Cost for part to construct twenty motor generators is $85,000 plus operational expenditure of $26,000.

This means our total budget for this project is $335,000 and if you divide this number by $500 we only need to issue 670 shares to a prospective investor's.

Stage 3

If enough funds are arranged and once proof-of concept passes testing okay, we will lodge a worldwide patent, attend various trade shows, to target motor and generator manufacturers. Budget is around $250,000.

Ricks

When it comes to the fulfillment of my project we have an engineer (William Donachie) who's on hand and has machining, welding and parts construction skills means this engineering side of this project is covered by our engineer.

Any machinery that comes from overseas will delay our project by up to six weeks.

Before we can start development a permit is required. However, before approval is granted, our workshop walls and ceiling may require sound proofing.

Marketing Plan

Following are our market position, pricing, and product margin structures. We plan to review them every six months in order to ensure that potential profits are

Products

ScorpiGem Limited is developing the following products:

Our company trades as Fluid Extreme Technologies is developing the following products:

Quad Core Mini-PC will sell for $799 considering most people do not need mid-range or high- end PCs now that cost over $1500.

AV500 Powerline Pass-through Starter Kits;

Turns your existing powerline into a high speed network No need for new wires or drilling, No configuration required simply plug your adapter into your power socket Integrated power socket for pass- through use

Speeds up to 500Mbps across 300 metres over household electrical wires.

ScorpiGem branded 55inch (3840*2160) UHD Television with USB, HDM1, VGA and DVBT. These will sell for $1,295 (Inc. GST) and come with 3 year factory backed warranty.

Surplustronics (an Auckland based electronics supplier) supplies us with power cables and dc connectors this allows us to greatly extend the distance of wireless security cameras.

DC Solar Battery Controller Charger.

This device has an output of @30 amps and feeds power to batteries and inverters. It will sell for $259.99 and it has a net profit of $78.54 per unit.

Why is this device better than the completion's versions? Well it comes with a separate 100v to 240v to 12v power supply. When solar power (at night time) goes out the power supply continuously feeds electricity the batteries that way they are kept topped up at night.

Motor Controller has an output of up to 30 amps.

This device not only feeds DC motors power to motor's but it also cycle magnetic fields too. This device will be targeted at motor manufacturers around the world and will not be sold on the retail market. The idea is to reduce the cost of DC motor controllers worldwide.

Competitors

Jaycar

They sell solar controllers for $309 to $1625, but they don't have any support for AC to DC battery charging, where our model does.

Noel Leeming Group

The Warehouse Group has acquired Noel Leeming Group from Gresham Private Equity effective from the 10th December 2012. For further information please see The Warehouse Group's media release.

"Noel Leeming Group" is a nationwide chain currently consisting of more than 80 retail stores.

Noel Leeming is Noel Leeming Group's flagship retail brand. It offers a superior standard of service and a broad range of branded consumer technology and appliances.

The Group's retail heritage extends over 100 years. During that period a solid foundation has been laid from which to grow business in to new and complementary areas.

Harvey Norman

Has become a household name and everyone is familiar with the slogan 'Go Harvey, Go Harvey, Go Harvey Norman'. This company motto, much like the supporting anthem for a favourite sporting team, conveys the enthusiasm and entrepreneurial spirit embedded in the Franchise operators and the Harvey Norman culture.

Same goes for Surplustronics an Auckland electronics supplier. Their models sell for $180 but they don't have an LED display, like our model and they also have no support AC to DC battery charging either.

In a future date (providing we have to funds), is to build a prototype of our high-tech Torq Velocity motor/Generator. It uses graphene and lasers to generate a stronger magnetic field and it also eliminates carbon brushes too.

Market research

Facts about your industry:

Some barriers to enter this market with your company: Low capital costs Low production costs.

Consumer acceptance and brand recognition shipping costs of electronic parts Tariff barriers and quotas.

We will take on these barriers as and when they occur, it's all about negotiation.

We are ready to adapt to the following that may affect our company?

Change in technology - now that 'graphene has been proved', it allows us to target high energy power users worldwide.

Changes to internet and the introduction of smart phones allow us to target potential purchasers via Google, Facebook and Twitter, etc.

Most PC System costs between $1,500 to over $2,000 to purchase this type of system. But your system is $599. Means users will save around $1,000. This could increase your sales.

We have identified that in order to compete again your competition, your prices will have to be better than them. Also your price for 55" ultra HD television is very good, and a 3 years warranty means customers could be very happy, if one happens to fail that is.

Change in the economy.

Change in your industry.

Sales Strategy.

Our generator will save people energy; meaning they can save lots as this device reduces energy consumption!

As such, the target market segments to focus on are small communities, and current gas-turbine generator manufacturers, because of the special market characteristics.

Positioning

Our products will target home users and small business users alike, which is easy to install, and now that powerline technology is available. It now means no more networking cables to install, which befits all of our clients.

One of our plans is to offer Mini PC purchasers 12 months interest free finance and a low deposit of 100 dollars. That's $83.25 per month or $19.25 per week.

So times that by ten people, generates $832.5 per month.

The generator will target home users and corporate users alike and it is designed to reduce greenhouse gas emissions worldwide too.

Mini PCs, powerline target home, and business users around the New Zealand wide.

Our products target home users, corporate users is easy to install, and now that powerline technology is available. It now means no more networking cables to install, which befits all of our clients.

One of our plans is to offer Mini PC purchasers 12 months interest free finance with a low deposit of 100 dollars.

First benefit of using this generator technology is that it can be used to extract hydrogen from water, as right now, the electrolysis process is far too expensive and solar power generation is too limited. There you go first problem solved.

About Global warming and climate change

(Information sourced from Wikipedia.com)

Are terms for the observed century-scale rise in the average temperature of the Earth's climate system and its related effects? Multiple lines of scientific evidence show that the climate system is warming. Many of the observed changes since the 1950s are unprecedented over tens to thousands of years.

In 2014 the United Nations Intergovernmental Panel on Climate Change (IPCC) Fifth Assessment Report concluded that "It is extremely likely that human influence has been the dominant cause of the observed warming since the mid-20th century." The largest human influence has been emission of greenhouse gases such as carbon dioxide, methane and nitrous oxide; human activities have led to carbon dioxide concentrations above levels not seen in hundreds of thousands of years. Climate model projections summarized in the report indicated that during the 21st century the global surface temperature is likely to rise a further 0.3 to 1.7 °C (0.5 to 3.1 °F) for their lowest emissions scenario and 2.6 to 4.8 °C (4.7 to 8.6 °F) for the highest emissions scenario. These findings have been recognized by the national science academies of the major industrialized nations and are not disputed by any scientific body of national or international standing.

Future climate change and associated impacts will differ from region to region around the globe. Anticipated effects include warming global temperature, rising sea levels, changing precipitation, and expansion of deserts in the subtropics. Warming is expected to be greater over land than over the oceans and greatest in the Arctic, with the continuing retreat of glaciers, permafrost and sea ice. Other likely changes include more frequent extreme weather events including heat waves, droughts, heavy rainfall with floods and heavy snowfall; ocean acidification; and species extinctions due to shifting temperature regimes. Effects significant to humans include the threat to food security from decreasing crop yields and the abandonment of populated areas due to rising sea levels. Because the climate system has a large "inertia" and greenhouse gases will stay in the atmosphere for a long time, many of these effects will not only exist for decades or centuries, but will persist for tens of thousands of years.

Possible societal responses to global warming include mitigation by emissions reduction, adaptation to its effects, building systems resilient to its effects, and possible future climate engineering. Most countries are parties to the United Nations Framework Convention on Climate Change (UNFCCC), whose ultimate objective is to prevent dangerous anthropogenic climate change. Parties to the UNFCCC have agreed that deep cuts in emissions are required and that global warming should be limited to well below 2.0 °C (3.6 °F) relative to pre-industrial levels,[b] with efforts made to limit warming to 1.5 °C (2.7 °F).

Public reactions to global warming and concern about its effects are also increasing. A global 2015 Pew Research Center report showed a median of 54% consider it "a very serious problem". There are significant regional differences, with Americans and Chinese (whose economies are responsible for the greatest annual CO2 emissions) among the least concerned. The generator will target home users and corporate users alike and it is designed to reduce greenhouse gas emissions worldwide too.

First benefit of using this generator technology is that it can be used to extract hydrogen from water, as right now, the electrolysis process is far too expensive and solar power generation is too limited. There you go first problem solved.

One of our targets is the Auckland New Zealand market, which is suffering from constant power outages. Using our motor/generator will people in Auckland not only to save electricity but our device if power goes out can automatically switch over to back up battery mode Once power is back on the controller automatically recharges the batteries. They can all have the satisfaction of knowing that their houses are not left in darkness, greenhouse gas emissions are lowered and the knowledge they can wash their clothes and also keep the freezers going.

Returns and Adjustments Policy

All products come with a twelve month warranty period. However, once the period has ended, we plan to offer end users with a repair service and this will cost them $50 to $150 plus GST per hour to fix faulty products.

Objectives

ScorpiGem Technology Limited Limited's overall advertising and promotional objectives are to: Position ScorpiGem Technology Limited as the leader in the energy industry.

Increase company awareness and brand name (ScorpiGem™) recognition among customers. Sell Mini and Micro personal computers, NZ wide.

Sell powerline networking products NZ Wide.

55inch (3840*2160) UHD Television with USB, HDMI, VGA and DVBT.

Advertising and Promotion

We plan to market and promote through the following: Stuff

online.

      Local newspapers. Trademe promotion.

      One option for us is to book space at the Ellerslie Event Centre in Auckland by offer our products are discounted prices to home users and business users.

However, the cost for this would be around $75,000, which includes advertising on radio and in newspapers. Since we get great deals from our suppliers we can reduce our prices without losing to much money.

Press Release

      We plan to send out press releases in Australian United States, United Kingdom, and New Zealand.

Trade Shows

      ScorpiGem Limited will only participate in the following trade shows:

Hannover Germany

Energy Show, Hannover Fairgrounds, Hannover, Germany CEBIT HANNOVER, Hannover Fairgrounds, Hannover, Germany.

Sydney Australia

    Energy Show.

Financial Plan

Financial projections are based on the following assumptions:

The Generator technology will generate profits.

Our financial projections are based on the following assumptions: Our security technology will generate profits:

Our sales forecast for first year is $17,357 per month. Our first year's expenditure will be $9,672 per month.

Total budget for advertising and promotion is $208 per month.

One of our plans is to offer Mini PC purchasers 12 months interest free finance and a low deposit of 100 dollars. That's $83.25 per month or $19.25 per week.

So times that by 10 people, generates $832.5 per month.

Financial Statements
Are available online.

We do expect to make a first years profit of $69,691 and for the second year is expected to be around $82,000. However, we do expect third year profit to rise to $103,896 as we will be moving into selling televisions on the New Zealand market.

We expect to sell around 250 ScorpiGem branded 55inch (3840*2160) UHD Television with USB, HDMI, VGA and DVBT. These will sell for $1,295 (Inc. GST) and come with 3 year factory backed warranty.

Primary Income-Related Items See

attached documentation

Gross Profit Analysis

The Gross Profit Analysis statements included in our Supporting Documents show yearly licence revenue, and gross profit values for each of our product lines for Years 2, 3 and 4.

The Gross Profit Analysis statements included in our Supporting Documents show yearly licence revenue, and gross profit values for each of our product lines for Years 1, and 2.

At $799 for a Windows 10 Mini PC package means users save money, even our Zorin Linux model will sell for $599 and our wireless keyboard with touch is great for the home theatre PC market and this system will sell for $399 to $599. So why pay over $1,000 for a PC that most users don't need. The other value of our Mini PCs is the you don't have send a monitor back for warranty reasons that's why don't recommend that people buy an all=in-one computer as they have to be sent back for warranty.

The solar battery charger controller would sell for around $259.99 per unit and will help consumers using solar panels to reduce their energy consumption by about fifty per cent. It's also easy to make due to its modular design as well.

Cash Flows Statements

At this early stage we can only project (Cash flow statements) on an annual basis for Years 1 to 4 as above.

Budget for West End Technologies Limited

Income		Weekly From August	Weekly (Future)	Monthly			
Other		$ 210.13	$ 210.13				
Loan From BNZ				$ 0.00	$ 0.00	$ 61,788.76	
Flexi Wage				$ 1,321.67	$ 15,860.00	$ 15,860.00	
Accommodation Supplement		$ 59.00	$ 59.00	$ 236.00	$ 2,832.00		
	Tax		$ 0.00	$ 149.61	$ 1,795.33		
	Total	$ 269.13	$ 269.13	$ 1,408.06	$ 16,896.68	$ 77,648.76	

Expenditure				One-off	
Marketing and Promotion				$ 2,385.74	
Marketing Materials				$ 87.96	
Talk2 internet phone account				$ 120.00	
Web hosting				$ 239.66	
NZ Company registration				$ 160.22	
NZ Companies Office annual fee				$ 90.00	
PNCC Certificates of compliance				$ 448.00	
Office Supplies				$ 472.98	
Machinery House				$ 74.76	
Clothing + footware				$ 746.31	
Stock				$ 37,880.18	
Startup					
Computer parts, etc				$ 2,246.19	
Refund				$ 1,361.76	Loan
Bank fees				$ 15,475	$ 50,000.00
Own funds				$ 0.00	
	Balance	$ 0.00	$ 0.00	$ 61,788.76	

Other Expences				
Board		$ 220.00	$ 880.00	
GE Money		$ 70.00	$ 280.00	
Doctor + Drugs		$ 0.00	$ 28.33	
Personal Expences		$ 0.00	$ 100.00	
	Total	$ 290.00	$ 1,288.33	

	Net Profit/Loss	-20.87		$ 119.72	← Red indicates a loss

			Tax $ 17.30			
	Projected Sales					
$ 44,047.00	Monitors					
$ 0.00	Mini PC	$ 4,368.00				
$ 3,250.00	Other					
$ 1,450.00	Mouse & Keyboard					
$ 520,500.00	TVs		$ 1,470.00	$ 325.33		
$ 209,872.00	Net Income	$ 55.81				
				Share Price	Capital Raised	
$ 271,660.76	← Company Value			$ 271.66	$ 67,915.19	250
	Manawatu Standard	Google	NZ Herald	Dominion Post		
	$ 1,211.09	$ 0.00	$ 1,174.66	$ 0.00		
$ 9.99						

			Cost	RRP	Profit	
	USD	NZD				
	$ 23,057.50		$ 619.14	$ 799.00	$ 179.86	← Windows 10
$ 46,000.00	$ 158,837.00					
			$ 0.00	$ 599.00	$ 599.00	← Zorin Linux
Overdraft	Stock Finance	Total				
$ 0.00	$ 0.00	$ 50,000.00	$ 500	$ 833	$ 4,975.00	
				Expenditure	Capital + Income	Net
-$ 7,265.57	← Balance of one-off expenditure			$ 127,648.76	$ 120,383.19	-$ 7,265.57

is a loss

Balance sheet 2016/2017 for West End Technologies Limited

	Dec 12	Jan 1	Feb 2	Mar 3	Apr 4	May 5	Jun 6	Jul 7	Aug 8	Year 1
	$ 11,391.44	$ 11,391.44	$ 11,391.44	$ 11,391.44	$ 11,391.44	$ 11,391.44	$ 11,391.44	$ 11,391.44	$ 11,391.44	$ 125,305.88
	$ 0.00	$ 0.00	$ 0.00	$ 0.00	$ 0.00	$ 0.00	$ 0.00	$ 0.00	$ 0.00	$ 0.00
	$ 60,191.59	$ 30,096.90	$ 60,191.59	$ 60,191.59	$ 60,191.59	$ 60,191.59	$ 60,191.59	$ 60,191.59	$ 60,191.59	$ 601,915.95
	$ 71,583.04	**$ 41,487.24**	**$ 71,583.04**	**$ 71,583.04**	**$ 71,583.04**	**$ 71,583.04**	**$ 71,583.04**	**$ 71,583.04**	**$ 71,583.04**	**$ 727,221.83**
	$ 0.00	$ 0.00	$ 0.00	$ 0.00	$ 0.00	$ 0.00	$ 0.00	$ 0.00	$ 0.00	$ 51,788.76
	$ 1,416.28	$ 1,416.28	$ 1,416.28	$ 1,416.28	$ 1,416.28	$ 1,416.28	$ 1,416.28	$ 1,416.28	$ 1,416.28	$ 122,397.32
	$ 114.22	$ 114.22	$ 114.22	$ 114.22	$ 114.22	$ 114.22	$ 114.22	$ 114.22	$ 114.22	$ 15,579.04
	$ 1,530.50	$ 1,530.50	$ 1,530.50	$ 1,530.50	$ 1,530.50	$ 1,530.50	$ 1,530.50	$ 1,530.50	$ 1,530.50	$ 1,256.42
									$ 191,021.53	**$ 191,021.53**
	$ 1,288.33	$ 1,288.33	$ 1,288.33	$ 1,288.33	$ 1,288.33	$ 1,288.33	$ 1,288.33	$ 1,288.33	$ 1,288.33	$ 15,460.00
										$ 400.00
										$ 0.00
										$ 0.00
										$ 50,000.00
	$ 33.33	$ 33.33	$ 33.33	$ 33.33	$ 33.33	$ 33.33	$ 33.33	$ 33.33	$ 33.33	$ 150,024.08
	$ 70,019.21	**$ 39,923.41**	**$ 70,019.21**	**$ 70,019.21**	**$ 70,019.21**	**$ 70,019.21**	**$ 70,019.21**	**$ 70,019.21**	**$ 70,019.21**	**$ 70,019.21**
	$ 55,742.42	$ 95,666.83	$ 166,685.64	$ 236,704.25	$ 305,723.46	$ 375,742.67	$ 445,761.87	$ 466,781.08	$ 365,776.21	$ 150,024.08
										$ 365,776.21

Milestones

Year 1 (2017/2018) Sell Mini personal computers, and powerline networking products NZ wide. Year 2 (2019/2020) Target AMD Zen base dual core APU with Radeon GPU at Gamers, NZ Wide.

Our overall advertising and promotional objectives are to: Position as the leader in the consumer electronics industry.

Break-Even Analysis

Our Break-Even Sales level for Year 1 is $100,621. This means we only need to sell 197 units per annum to make a profit.

Manufacturing licence fee on all sales: 8% pa. Royalty

fee on all sales: 15% per product.

Capital Requirements

Our business needs $250,000 is needed to develop our new electronic, PC and networking business.

Use of Funds

Marketing and Promotion - Prnz, Google & Stuff, Marketing Materials, Voip business phone line, setup webhosting account, registration our company, pay PNCC for a certificate of compliance, purchase printer ink, and paper. Order computer chair. In addition, stock has to be ordered as well.

Import our very own ScorpiGem branded 55inch (3840*2160) UHD Televisions into New Zealand to sell them via our own website and also through Trademe.

Conclusion

Why we will be successful, ScorpiGem Limited enjoys an expression of satisfaction and encouragements are numerous, and we intend to take advantage of this to grow in the marketplace with more unique and effective products. Based on the attached financial projections, we believe that this venture represents a sound business proposition.

Miscellaneous Documents:

Gen Townsley CV.

William Donachie CV.

Personal financial statements.

Business financial statements

Supplier Quotes.

Product Information.

Miscellaneous relevant documents.

Products

Windows 10 Linux Mini PC - $799.00 With Monitor CT230 AMD Kabini 5200M Radeon R5 Mini-PC with 8GB ram, 128GB SSD and Windows 10 Home x64

    1TB external portable USB hard drive.

    24" 16:9 Business LED Monitor, 1920x1080, HDMI, Speaker and 3 Years perfect panel warranty

    2.4G wireless keyboard and mouse with black/white.

Upgrade Options:

Slim Portable Blu-Ray Writer & DVD Writer, Black Color $149.00

Vesa adapter bracket - 75/100mm to 200/400mm $19.00

2TB external portable USB 3.0 hard drive $209.

27" 16:9 Business LED Monitor, 2560x1440, HDMI, Displayport, Speaker, 3 Years perfect panel warranty $449 (upgrade $229).

Classical black universal desktop wireless Bluetooth keyboard $29.

Slim Portable Blu-Ray Writer & DVD Writer, Black Color $129.

28" 16:9 4K LED Monitor, 3860x2160, HDMI, Displayport, Speaker, 3 Years perfect panel warranty $499.00.

Networking

AV500 Powerline Adapter with inbuilt 300MbAV500 WiFi Extender $69.

--end of book--

www.ingramcontent.com/pod-product-compliance
Lightning Source LLC
Chambersburg PA
CBHW061451180526
45170CB00004B/1664